To my students for not only teaching me that love is the most excellent tool a teacher can use in the classroom but also for being a constant source of inspiration.

To my family and friends for sustaining me always.

Special thanks to Kirk, Carmen, Alliyah, Tiffany, and Daphne for reading for me.

I love you all!

Foreward

After years of working as a sports writer and then in the advertising industry, I returned to school to become a teacher. On my first day of teaching, I walked into an environment plagued by pain, fear, and anger after experiencing overwhelming community trauma.

During the year that followed, I realized that my college education had not prepared me for the classroom. I discovered that the education system does not work in the best interest of the children. And, I realized that the relationships with my students were more important than anything else.

In March of 2020, the country locked down in response to the COVID-19 outbreak. We all went home for spring break and we never went back to school that year. I did not get to see my students play ball or attend prom or cross the stage at graduation. In fact, I never saw some of them again. The disconnection from my kids traumatized me. I still had so much more to share with them.

This book is a continuation of the conversations we started that year but never finished. I am sure there will be more to say even after this.

But for now, I love you all. I hope you are well. And I hope you never forget that you matter.

Love, Ms. Rausch

Chapter One

You matter.

"You are not a drop in the ocean. You are the entire ocean in a drop." — Rumi

You matter.

You are significant.

Your existence in this world is of paramount importance.

You are the living legacy of every human being in your bloodline who came before you.

You are the intention behind the hard work and determination, and survival of your ancestors.

You are the hope of generations to come and the aspirations of all of us who tried but did not get it quite right.

And, you matter.

More specifically, you matter to me. I know, I know… You are probably thinking that it is impossible to matter to someone who does not even know you. You might even be thinking that if I really knew you, I would not be saying that you mattered. But I assure you, it is true. You matter to me.

I have been saying this for a while now: if the world is going to truly change, it is young people who will change it. It is you who will lead crowds of people out of the darkness and into the light of a world that is accepting and loving, and kind, where equality exists without discussion, opportunity is endless, and joy supersedes want in the lives of every human being. That might sound like a tall order, but you are up to the task. I know this because I know you… or people like you… and I believe in your power and ability.

When I started to write this book, I did it because teenagers changed my life. At the age of 38, I returned to college to get my master's degree in education, thinking that I would go out and change the world and make it a better place for future generations. But it was me who changed. My world was reshaped and reconstructed in a way I never anticipated. My students made me a better person. They taught me about life and love and fear and resilience in ways I had never been exposed to before, and they made it ok for me to truly be myself for the first time in my life without fear of judgment or retribution.

So I wanted to make sure that I paid that forward in some way. This book is part of that. By the time I left the classroom to teach in new ways, on larger platforms, and in bigger spaces, I realized two things. One, as an educator, the relationships one develops with students are essential to any potential success as a teacher and the students' success in life. And, two, I loved my kids, and I wanted to teach them so much more than I ever got to say, but importantly, I wanted them to soar, be successful, and live long and happy lives.

Since relationships are the foundation of everything, your contribution to the world, no matter how big or small, is critical and unique. I cannot be me without you. I cannot do what I do or live how I live without the other people in the world who make that possible, whether they know that or not. That includes you.

For example, if I want to bake a cake from scratch, I must collect ingredients like eggs. I need the farmers who cultivate the land and grow corn fed to chickens who lay the eggs to bake that cake. Somewhere, you fit into a chain of events that make some things possible. You exist for a reason. And, you matter.

When I was a little girl, my dad loved to put together puzzles. Sometimes our whole family would sit around the dining room table and work the pieces attempting to connect a corner or a block of four, six, or eight pieces. My dad taught us to find all the pieces with flat edges first because they made up the border of the puzzle. The border framed the picture we were constructing. And that frame supported every other connection we made. However, if we did not have the border built first, it was more challenging to piece it together, but also it often made it impossible to determine where a cluster of pieces should be placed in the center.

Similarly, the circle of people we choose to have around us either supports us, enlightens us, and helps us to be more successful in our lives, or it leaves us wandering, seeking out connections in the wrong places, and wondering where we fit in the world or even just in our small community like the neighborhoods where we live, our schools, our churches, or our jobs.

Now, more than once, my dad reached the end of a puzzle, and two or three pieces would be missing. In that case, it was impossible to produce a complete picture which led to frustration and some cursing. Without all of the pieces, the puzzle was not a whole picture. It was broken. It had gaping holes. And sometimes, an entire section of the border was missing, leaving the puzzle unsupported and at risk of falling apart.

The same goes for a world without you. It is incomplete. Without you, entire communities like your family, friend group, church, job, and school would be vulnerable. They would be weaker, not whole, and unhealthy. Predestined connections would not happen, not just for you but for others with whom you were supposed to connect or who you were supposed to help connect to others.

Whether you know it or not, you have been intentionally created with unique skills and abilities that only you can perform in the way you were created to do so. For example, there might be 101 people who are great in a crisis, but nobody solves problems precisely like you.

Imagine this for a moment: we are at a dinner party, seated at a long dining room table. Twelve chairs are lined up on each side, and one is at each end. You and I are sitting shoulder-to-shoulder in the first and second chairs, but there is no one else on our side of the table. On the other side of the table, a friend or family member or someone else from our inner circle is seated in every chair. (The twelve chairs on the other side of the table are full.) Before we begin eating, someone asks you to pass the salt and pepper beside your plate. Gladly, you pick up the salt and pepper and pass it to me, and then we all continue passing the salt and pepper around the table until they are received by the person who requested them.

"Thank you!" they cheerfully yell from the far

end of the room. You smile and say, "You're welcome." They return the smile.

Your role in that transaction was minor but impactful. You willingly lent a helping hand. Your good deed invoked a warm response. They enjoyed their dinner much more because of your kindness. And it's scientifically proven that a smile can change someone's entire day by shifting their demeanor and their emotions from a negative space to a positive space. (Do you know how powerful you are?)

Could someone else have stood up or reached across the table to get the salt and pepper? Absolutely. But they did not have to because you were there. It might be a silly story, but we are frequently positioned in the right place at the right time. When we step into that space wholly and authentically, we fulfill a purpose or a role. And it might be as uncomplicated as passing the salt, but it could also be as big as changing the world.

The gifts and talents bestowed upon you are uniquely yours, designed to impact the world in a profoundly YOU kind of way. Nobody works like you. Nobody loves like you. Nobody else shows up like you.

You matter because you are a piece of the bigger picture! You fill a gap in our existence. You might even be a corner piece in the border or a cornerstone in the foundation. Without you, possibilities are no longer endless. They are limited. I cannot do this life without you. None of us can.

To be completely transparent, as a young person, I often wondered what the point of my life was. There are still days now when I question my purpose on earth and whether or not I have impacted the world in a big enough way or if I have achieved enough success. And if I made a list of everything good that I have done in my life or if I measured my wins against my losses, the evidence would demonstrate that I have done alright. But you could stack evidence to the ceiling, and it wouldn't prevent self-doubt from creeping in now and then.

Quite a few years ago, I sold my house and everything I owned and moved back into the house where I grew up. My parents were getting older, and my mom's diagnosis of Alzheimer's was growing and changing in a way that made caring for her complex for my dad sometimes. I went home to help. While it might not seem like a monumental decision to go home and care for an ailing parent, doing so dramatically changes every aspect of life. I resented my family for expecting me to care for my parents. And I hated life sometimes. Oftentimes, boiling anger would bubble up inside of me, and I would verbally explode. I felt like I didn't matter, like what I wanted didn't matter, like the plans I had for my life didn't matter. I felt like nobody heard me when I shared what I needed, and if they did listen to me, I felt like they did not care.

But I absolutely mattered. People told me all the time that they thought I was a great daughter or that they could never do what I was doing. My parents thanked me. And sometimes, my mom would say, "I love you, Michele," five or six times before she finally went to sleep at night.

My inner voice and my sense of regret were battling with my reality, and some days, traumas of the past were manifesting in ways that were hurtful to those around me. It was not that I did not matter. It was that I felt like I didn't matter, and I had to find ways to deal with those feelings instead of lashing out at my parents or the other people around me.

Sometimes, we get stuck in the muck and the mire of everyday dramas, traumas, and struggles. It is easy to fall into pitfalls of self-doubt or situations that drain our confidence, especially if the people around us are a source of negativity.

Honestly, some of your situations might be pretty desperate. You could be in the midst of your trauma right now, dealing with unimaginable hardships from homelessness and food insecurity to abuse to the loss of friends and loved ones who have succumbed to substance abuse or died by gun violence or whose lives have been changed by incarceration. And you are in the midst of trying to figure out who you are or what path you are going to take.

And the darkness and the depth of a crisis, no matter how trivial it may seem to other people, can feel like being buried alive. The more you dig, the more dirt gets thrown on you. And sometimes it feels like you are digging with a spoon when what you really need is a bulldozer.

Progress feels slow or stagnant because you not only do not have the support of the people in your life, but you don't have adequate tools or resources for success. It is like building a house without a blueprint or without ever being taught how to swing a hammer properly. (But we can talk about that more later.)

I promise you that on the other side of the darkness is light. On the other side of the uncertainty is confidence. On the other side of lack is abundance. On the other side of loneliness is the fearlessness to dominate when you have to work alone. Just keep digging. Brush that dirt off of your shoulders and keep working. There is rest up ahead.

It is natural to allow the influence of those around us, especially our family members or others with whom we are close to weigh heavily as we gather the information that helps us build our core beliefs about ourselves. We often allow the measure of our worth or our value to rest in the hands of others. And if those points of view or opinions are negative (or not self-esteem building), we do not always have enough know-how or self-determination to overcome them. So we buy the bill of goods they are selling. They know better. They have lived longer. They have more background. But I call bullshit on that. I see you. And you matter.

About a year before my mom died in April of 2022, almost to the exact day, she was getting ready to head into her room to go to bed. We had been watching television together, and as she pulled herself up and grabbed her walker, she took a few steps toward me and stopped.

Our "good nights" to one another took a little while sometimes because Mom was chatty like me. I was sitting on one end of the couch, lazily slouched against the arm, scrolling through some social media app. My mom looked down at me and told me how lucky she felt to have my sister, my dad, and me in her life. She teased me about how I do things around the house.

She said, "We all have our own way of doing things." And I agreed. But before she left, she said what was probably the nicest thing anyone had ever said to me. She said, "Thank you for being who you are." I can still hear her saying it. That one sentence was simple yet profound and powerful.

"Thank you for being who you are" is all-inclusive. "Who you are" is **_all_** of you, every part of you, nothing left out.

She did not say, "Thank you for being kind," or "Thank you for being so easy to get along with," or "Thank you for…" anything specific. She did not thank me for being just the things that are easy to love or for being just the things that she liked about me. She thanked me for being WHO I AM. All of who I am is worthy of love. All of who I am is something to be thankful for. All of who I am… matters.

And so I say the same to you.

THANK YOU FOR BEING WHO YOU ARE.

You matter.

<u>All of you</u> matters.

You matter simply because you exist.

"You are imperfect, you are wired for struggle, but you are worthy of love and belonging." —Brene Brown

Chapter Two

Never stop learning.

"Wisdom is not a product of schooling but of the lifelong attempt to acquire it." Albert Einstein

Be curious.

Ask questions.

Read.

Try new things.

Talk to people you think you have nothing in common with or who seem like they could not be more different than you.

Eat foods you have never heard of or don't look like something you would eat.

Follow directions.

Listen to the world around you. Pay attention to how it lives and breathes, and moves.

Never stop learning.

Before you continue reading, I need to issue a warning: I will talk about school in this chapter. BUT

PLEASE KEEP READING. Because learning is not reserved for the classroom. It is more significant than that.

Admittedly, as a teacher, I believe in the power of a bountiful education. Books arm readers with information and ideas. Literature empowers the imagination and sparks creative thinking. Reading opens the doors of possibilities and adventure, and escape. It also makes us better writers and speakers. It shows us cultures unlike our own and enlightens our understanding of each other.

When we read (if it is a good book that grabs our attention and holds it til the last page or allows us to connect in some way), the story transports us to other places in the world, affords us the opportunity to time travel, and introduces us to people we might never have known. Likewise, other content areas unlock otherwise unopened parts of the brain, stimulating strategic thinking, problem-solving, innovation, and invention and fostering social skills, empathy, and emotional growth.

Our brains continue to grow through the age of 25. Everything we learn creates a connection in our brain or unlocks the potential of a part of our brain to operate at total capacity. But if we do not learn, we do not open our brains up to whatever comes next. It is like putting a cake pan in the oven and hoping to pull out a fully baked cake 30 minutes later without ever pouring batter into the pan.

It is difficult to understand why teachers force you to learn things that do not seem useful or do not seem like something you will need in the future. But education aims to build skills you can apply to other areas of your life. For example, community-building exercises in the classroom, like working in groups or reading in a circle, enhance your communication skills, prepare you for collaborating with others in everyday situations, and often give you the opportunity to figure out how to overcome the challenge of having teammates who do not pull their own weight. Group activities might ignite your desire to lead or force you to figure out where you fit in various scenarios. (Everyone has something to offer in those situations, too, whether you realize it or not.)

Also, scientific studies show that learning occurs when connections are made in the brain. The more you do something, the stronger those connections get, increasing the chance that whatever that thing is will become ingrained in your brain, so it will be easier to recall and easier to complete over time.

Here is an example: if you walk or drive to the same place every day, eventually, you don't have to think about how to get there. You automatically follow the route to your destination without thinking too hard about it. But when you have to try something for the first time, your brain has to work harder to complete that new task.

How many of you ever watched Dora the Explorer? Remember how Dora repeated everything over and over, and she even asked you to recall what she said? Eventually, you could anticipate when she would gather up her backpack, and you could sing the backpack song with her. You knew when she would turn to the map for assistance, and you could sing the map song too.

"Over the hill, through the woods,

across the river!"

"Over the hill, through the woods,

across the river!"

"Over the hill, through the woods,

across the river!"

The repetition and your engagement in Dora's adventure created a more robust connection in your brain, allowing you to remember key points throughout the show.

So what do all those core classes teach you? Well, math unlocks your analytical brain. It teaches you to think critically and builds the connections in your brain needed to think logically in various situations.

English enhances your communication skills, bolstering your writing, speaking, listening, and reading abilities which are necessary skills in any profession. And, incidentally, the more you read, the better you will get at it. (Remember… just like Dora… repetition is the key to mastery.) English classes also teach you how to reason, strategize, analyze, make connections, imagine, infer, ask questions… and much more.

Science, by definition, is learning through practice. (That's why they say doctors "practice" medicine.) In science class, you learn about the importance of safety and planning, and preparedness. Science sparks your curiosity, makes you more inquisitive, and helps create a path to potential answers.

History... Well, if we learn actual history, it should show us what not to do, help us learn from the mistakes of those who came before us, and how to create the world we want to live in... But that is just my two cents.

Socialization is a huge part of education too. Learning how to cultivate relationships and associate with people outside of your family circle begins when you step into school for the first time. Adapting to new rules or different ways of doing things is a part of it, as well as time management and fulfilling responsibilities. And all of that is just the tip of the iceberg.

School might not feel practical to you. There will be days when you really cannot connect the lesson to real life. But I promise you the connection is there.

I firmly believe in formal education or school because I know the benefits of it if the environment is safe, inclusive, and conducive to learning.

Look, I know that college is not for everyone. But many people might have said that about me. When I entered my senior year, I could either get a full-time job or attend school. I chose school mainly because I did not want to work and because I wanted to keep playing ball.

However, I am glad I made that decision. College presented the ultimate struggle for a kid who hated school but needed to pass twelve credits a semester to stay there.

It took me seven years to get my undergraduate degree. I partied a lot. I got into a lot of trouble. I am not advocating that for others, but there were some incredible experiences during the craziness. I met so many people who I would never have met without college. Going to classes in a place where I did not know anybody forced me out of my comfort zone and demanded that I carve out an identity separate from where I came from or who my friends were.

Why not allow college to audition for you? Take one class and make sure it is a subject you really enjoy. See how it goes. And if it's not that great, go get some kind of training to enhance a skill or an interest you

have. Join a book club. Do something outside of your comfort zone. Whatever you do,
DO NOT JUST SIT AT HOME.

All that said, all education does not occur inside the walls of the traditional schoolhouse. Education or learning comes in a variety of occurrences beyond formal education too.

Experiences increase knowledge and understanding, but they also produce great stories. Some of that practice comes at home or in your family environment.

My mom taught me to cook at a very young age. By the time I was four years old, I could make pancakes by myself. I remember pushing a chair up to the counter and climbing up so I could assist with measuring the ingredients. My mom taught me how to read a recipe. Did you know that in a recipe, a small "t" (or a lowercase t) stands for "teaspoon," and a big "T" (or a capital T) stands for "Tablespoon?" If you did, it is likely that someone either taught you like my mom taught me or you learned that by reading. My mom also taught me how to level off dry ingredients in a measuring cup with a butter knife. She showed me how to whisk and stir and shake and fold and all of the other directions you might see in a recipe.

My dad taught me how to change a tire and check the oil on my first car. And then, on my first solo road trip, I learned how to call for help when my tire popped and unraveled on the highway in Miami, Oklahoma. I learned all by myself how to make decisions that would get me back home safely… because I had to…

Speaking of my first road trip, traveling provides an unmatched education. Travel. Travel. Travel. Seeing the world beyond the five-mile radius around your house, indulging in unfamiliar foods, meeting as many new people as possible, gazing across unfamiliar landscapes, participating in cultural activities that are not your own… That is the route to world peace, but it is also the path to an education you cannot get in your house, neighborhood, or school.

Traveling alone might require a bit of bravery, but it frees you from the limitations placed upon you by your friends and your family, who are not quite as adventurous and daring. Embracing that which is not like you through travel opens your heart, mind, and eyes in a way that makes home feel really vanilla, but it also enlightens your sense of possibility.

Escaping the status quo and venturing into new, unseen places offered me irreplaceable knowledge in my twenties and thirties. Of course, I still had to work full time by then, but much of my money went to seeing as much of our country as possible. The level of diversity in culture and food and religion and environment, and people in this country is abundantly more than you can imagine.

New York City is completely different from St. Louis, which is completely different from Los Angeles and Des Moines, and Miami and Milwaukee. How people get to work in cities across the United States varies based on the landscape, the efficiency of public transit, traffic, and the proximity of home to school and work. What people eat for breakfast is different from place to place. Where they spend their time is different. How they talk is different. IT IS THE MOST BEAUTIFUL THING IN THE WORLD.

Have you seen the people in Times Square in New York dressed as Elmo who take pictures for money? In LA, you can find impromptu food stands set up in front of folks' houses where you can get the BEST tacos made by somebody's mom. The smell of beer brewing in Milwaukee wafts across the breeze, and late at night, when people are leaving the clubs and the bars to go home, sausage stands are set up on the corners and, while it might have been heavily influenced by the beer, I might have had the best sausage I have ever had there.

Speaking of food and beer. TRY IT. Eat sushi. Go to a wine tasting. Dine at the new Indian restaurant in town. Make friends with your Pakistani neighbors and get invited to dinner! Don't limit yourself to chips and mozzarella sticks, and chicken tenders. Go into a Vietnamese establishment and ask them what you should order. Once a month, visit a restaurant or a food truck, or a festival you have never come across before and get an education through food and drink and getting to know people who are not like you.

You can also learn through volunteering which is the one thing that everyone can afford to do. I spent every month of my 40th year volunteering for a different cause, and it was the most rewarding year of my life. Serving the community exposed me to stories that aren't often told, or that rarely get the spotlight. Volunteering affords you the opportunity to examine your heart a little bit too. Learning about yourself can carry you all the way to your next adventure.

And when you have done all of that OR when all else fails, you can get a job.

Legitimate employment is ripe with lessons. You might learn that you never want to work for someone else again and that you want to start your own business. But I submit to you that jobs can be stepping stones to the future you want if you choose them wisely and you engage in the learning they provide.

It's no secret that I don't like to work in one place for too long. The same boredom that plagued me throughout my education rears its ugly head on the job. If I don't feel like I am still learning or growing, or if the experiences get stale (what others might call comfortable), I am out! Most people see that as a bad thing, but it has been a blessing for me. I have worked as a baker & a prep cook in a restaurant, a nanny, a public relations liaison, a sports writer, a publications coordinator, a technical writer, a project manager, a coach, and a teacher. I have been the low man in the seniority rankings, and I have been the boss. What I have discovered is that in all things, it's the people that matter most. It doesn't matter the job, the process, or the industry, working is really all about the people you will meet and the experiences you will have.

Every job I have had has been connected to the next. I have used the opportunities in each position to build toward the next position, whatever it would be. I did not have an end goal. I didn't even have a dollar amount I wanted to make. I just wanted to love my job and get paid for doing it, and eventually, I wanted to build a career from everything I lived through.

Having a job has taught me how to travel, how to tip in restaurants and at hotels or the airport. It has taught me how to engage with people I do not know by finding some common ground to strike up a conversation. It has taught me how to enhance what I know and use that to build business, build relationships, and ultimately make money.

So what if you are just floundering in life? You do not love your job. You may have given up on school or thought college was not for you. You want a change, but you are not sure how to do that now. Well, learn from your failures. We cannot truly win until we lose. We cannot succeed until we have failed. But it is never too late to try again. You might need a little more learnin'!

College is not just for 18-year-old fresh-faced freshmen, so you can always get that college career started. Vocational training doesn't have an age limit either. My advice would be to get a job in the industry you think you want to work in. Let's say you have always wanted to be a veterinarian or a veterinary tech working at the zoo. Why are you still working fast food, then? Get a job answering the phone at the veterinary office or working in a lab at the zoo. It might not be glamorous, but it will give you relevant information about the career you want, and it will be a stepping stone toward your future.

If you want to teach, get a job in a school. If you want to be a music producer, be a volunteer intern at a studio or under someone who has the knowledge you need. If you want to be a baseball scout, do not get a job working in the concession stand at the ballpark, get a job working in the front office for a professional team. You might have to make some sacrifices like getting up earlier or ceasing some recreational activities, but in the long run, it will be worth the education you receive.

NEVER STOP LEARNING.

Observe.

Listen.

Read.

Try.

Your life will be richer for it. (And your bank account might be too!)

"The beautiful thing about learning is nobody can take it away from you." -B.B. King

Chapter Three

You are not the worst thing that ever happened to you.

"I know it hurts. I know you feel like you weren't good enough. But your breakthrough is coming. Don't give up on yourself now. You came too far. Your value is still high, and you're still beautiful. You don't need anyone to claim you to feel whole. Let it hurt and grow from it."
— Keishorne Scott

You are not the thing that happened.
You are the bounce back.
You are the bounce forward.
You are not the pain.
You are determination.
You are strength.
You are everything it took to be right here,
right now, at this moment.
You are here.
And that's all the proof you need.

You are more than the worst thing that has ever happened to you. There are days when that doesn't feel true, especially if you are sitting right in the middle of it. But if there is one thing I know for sure about trauma and pain, it is that although our experiences are unique and we respond to them in our own way, we all have the capacity to establish a path forward from life-altering moments.

Trauma is very real and it affects us in very different ways. There are different types of trauma, but even if we all endure the exact same type of trauma in the exact same way, how it impacts us is going to be different from person to person to person.

In the same way that we respond to our traumatic experiences differently, how that trauma might manifest later in life can be distinctive as well. But it shows up in our relationships and at our jobs, in how we operate on a daily basis, the habits we develop, and how we deal with different situations. It might be explosive rage or a desire to curl up in a ball and hide. It can be seen in substance abuse or the inability to work toward a healthy relationship, or the struggle to keep a job. I have heard it said that trauma manifests in our reactions, and that is very true.

The brain is a complex character. I won't pretend to know even half of how it works, but I do know that every experience we have (negative or positive) creates a connection in the brain. Those connections facilitate learning, allow us to build skills and harness our talents, and make it possible for us to be successful in life. Trauma can interrupt those connections or prevent them altogether.

As babies, the connections in our brains are created by the love and care we receive from the people around us. Those connections define for us how certain behaviors get certain responses. When we cry, someone will pick us up or feed us, for example. However, if we aren't born into a loving environment where we are nurtured and cared for, those connections might not happen. Or, if we go through some kind of trauma during that time, those connections could be altered in some way, preventing our brain from developing healthily.

Trauma walks hand in hand through our lives with grief and loss, but sometimes it is all very difficult to recognize because they have either always been around or they show up disguised as our "normal" everyday life. In other words, if stress permeates our lives and we thrive in chaos, or we are in survival mode constantly, trauma might not feel very traumatic. For example, we might have moved a lot. Maybe every few years, we moved to a new home. That was a normal part of life. So we don't recognize it as a type of loss or see it as traumatic, so we don't call it that, and we don't see it as something we need to heal from or seek help with. But for others, that kind of uprooting proves challenging, and repeatedly starting over is traumatizing.

No matter your situation or how or where you grew up, trauma occurs. We experience loss. We grieve, or we just keep it moving. But it happens, and sometimes the emotions we feel might surprise us. The event doesn't have to be huge or dramatic to qualify for the title of trauma or loss, either.

Death and homelessness, and the lack of food are traumatic events. They are losses that create measurable sadness. But the end of a friendship qualifies too. Having a car repossessed, a change in your everyday routine, the lights getting cut off, being in an accident, missing a critical appointment, misplacing a prized possession or a gift from someone you love… They can all be counted as losses, and they can all trigger our grieving process.

On top of that, the trauma and the loss that happens to others can also affect us. Our parents' battles impact us, as do their losses and their traumas. When a parent goes through difficult times, it often makes parenting impossible, and their fear, anger, and pain trickles down onto their children. It is called vicarious trauma.

As a little girl, I witnessed the financial hardships my parents faced. My dad's job went on strike multiple times, which meant he could not work until the company and the employees reached an agreement on a new contract. And as long as he was not working, the paychecks did not come. Uncertainty about the future stressed out my parents which rolled down to us kids. We felt the pressure and the tension in the air. Our stress showed up in the form of temper tantrums and sibling arguments, which just created more strain in our home.

Stress piles up, creating a toxic environment. Within the example from my childhood, we recognize "loss" in my dad's loss of work and the loss of paychecks which eventually threatens financial security and could ultimately mean the inability to put food on the table or heat in the house. Those losses cause sadness or fear or anxiety, and maybe a host of other emotions. And all of that is traumatic for the parents and the children.

Your trauma is not your fault. Could it have been prevented? Maybe. Could life have been different? Possibly. But it wasn't. It happened. Unfortunately, you don't get to decide how it affects you. How it shows up in your life can be unpredictable. But you do have the choice to deal with it so it doesn't get in your way. You can influence it so it doesn't continue to mess up your life. You can develop strategies to help you regulate your behavior. You can engage in resources like therapy to work through the impact of your trauma and to figure out how you keep moving in spite of it. You can be successful. You can have healthy relationships. You can rediscover your passion or your motivation, or your desire to live a full and happy life. And you can stop being angry or sad or hopeless too.

Healing happens on a unique timeline determined by you, based on your needs. No two timelines are exactly the same, but your trauma does not have to define you.

When I was 28 years old, I found out I was pregnant. I was not married. I was not even in a committed relationship. My parents' disappointment in me was bigger than the fact that I was having a baby out of wedlock. It grew out of their sense of loss. They raised me to wait to have a family until I was married and the notion that their daughter could be bringing a child into the world without the benefit of a loving relationship hurt them. They thought there would be a wedding before the baby. And their grief revealed itself as anger and sorrow.

But I was not a kid! The father of my child was a professional baseball player. I knew we would be okay, at least financially. Also, I wanted nothing more than to be a mom, so I had no shortage of love for a baby. We were going to be fine. Until we were not fine.

Midway through my pregnancy, I started cramping and bleeding. My body fought to hold on to my baby long enough for him to be healthy. While my baby's father traveled out of town for the All-Star Game, I lay on the couch praying for my child to survive. But within days, contractions started, and it was just too early. I lost the baby. In an instant, my heart burst into a million little pieces. My hopes and dreams were shattered. Pain consumed me. I cried desperately for weeks. I could not imagine waking up ever again and feeling normal or good or right. Every year that I did not have another baby, the sadness grew deeper and deeper.

It took ten years for me to really be able to talk about it. And it was not until I became a teacher, working with kids, that my healing really began.

Of course, others wondered why I couldn't just get over it or why I held onto the pain and the loss and the trauma of losing a child. Many thought I should just move on or focus on something more positive. But my grief was mine to process. My loss was my burden to bear. I dictated the time I needed to mend my heart and rejuvenate my spirit. Nobody else could define that.

Pain may have been thrust upon you. You may not have had any choice in the suffering. You did not ask for the bad stuff to happen in your life. But you do get to decide to step over it or on it or through it to get to the other side. You do get to decide how to engage resources that can help on your healing journey. You do get to decide how long that healing takes.

You are not the worst thing that ever happened to you. You are not your trauma. You are not your pain. You are not the loss. You are not your grief. You are not the things.

You are magnificent.
You are worthy.
You are valuable.
You are bigger than the stuff.
You are the decision-maker on this healing journey.

"I am grounded in joy; I'm not grounded in the trauma anymore." Tarana Burke

Chapter Four

Don't forget to breathe.

"Breath is the bridge which connects life to consciousness, which unites your body to your thoughts. Whenever your mind becomes scattered, use your breath as the means to take hold of your mind again." *Thich Nhat Hanh*

When you are making a decision,
Don't forget to breathe.
When you are angry or upset,
Don't forget to breathe.
When the excitement of life is too much to handle,
Don't forget to breathe.
In all things, pause and reflect before you speak
or act.
And, don't forget to breathe.

I don't understand why my young people are racing through life. I mean, I do… There are a lot of reasons that we will dive into shortly. But I also don't understand why the adults around you aren't holding onto you tightly enough to allow you to experience a long, happy childhood. I feel like we have failed you because we should be guarding and protecting you from growing up too fast, from seeing the horrors of the world, from being forced into the responsibilities of adulthood, and from turning into… us.

So many of you are living life twenty years in advance of your actual age. I do realize there are many reasons pushing you to accelerate the timelines of your lives but, from my seat of experience, I see some of you being cheated of the chance to truly live.

Some kids have watched their friends die before the age of 18 or shortly thereafter. Others are consumed with these being the end times. Often, I hear young ladies longing for a baby because they want someone who is theirs, someone who will love them unconditionally, someone who won't leave them. Still, others long for independence from what they perceive as servitude under their parents. And finally, many are being prematurely pushed out of the nest by parents who no longer want the responsibility of their children.

I once heard my aunt tell my cousin that life is not supposed to be figured out, it is supposed to be lived and enjoyed. Pure genius! This notion occupies a great deal of time and space in my thoughts lately. What exactly does that mean?

While, for each of us, the path of truly living will vary and will absolutely lead in a unique direction, I can reflect on my beautiful life and offer some ideas that might also work for others.

The pressure to grow up is so intense these days. But you have so much life ahead of you. Live it a little. There's plenty of time to work 60 hours a week, buy a mansion, adopt seven dogs, and join the PTA. Slow down. And, LIVE life. But in order to do that, you have to pause and breathe. Don't. Forget. To. Breathe.

A few months ago, I was sitting in a virtual meeting. Everyone joined the meeting from different locations across the country, but we had been working together for quite a while. At one point, as I spoke passionately about an issue we were discussing, I became visibly emotional. The facilitator of the conversation stopped me. She said, "Michele, tell me what you are feeling right now." And, I could not find words to accurately describe how I felt.

So she said, "Ok, tell me how you are feeling physically. What is happening in your body right now?" Placing my hands on my chest, I responded, "I feel like I can't breathe."

That day, I discovered that in moments when I feel strongly about something or when I have too much on my plate, and I feel like I am rushing around, I sometimes hold my breath, or I breathe in such a shallow manner that it exhausts me. I also learned that sometimes, I need to pause and breathe deeply.

The world is a very different place than it was when I was growing up. Children remained children much longer than they do today. When I was twelve years old, I was still a little girl with very little exposure to adult things. I had plenty of time to breathe.

I had never kissed a boy, although I did have a crush on a couple of boys in my sixth-grade class. The internet had not been invented yet, so I had little, if any, connection to the world outside of my hometown. I had never seen a rated-R movie. I knew nothing about drugs of any kind. (Although, beer was a staple at our family gatherings, so I knew plenty about alcohol.) I never witnessed community violence.

My capacity to dream expanded daily because my innocence was protected by my parents and by the community around me. Dreaming is a luxury not afforded to everyone. I had the luxury of dreaming.

When we can't dream because we are so busy surviving, we also lose opportunities to just breathe. When we rush because we feel like we are running out of time, we also lose opportunities to breathe. When we hurry through our childhood so we can be grown and independent and do adult things, we lose opportunities to just breathe.

You might feel limited in life right now, like you don't have control over anything or like you aren't able to make any of your own decisions. You might be chasing freedom from childhood or the past. But life's limitations are temporary.

One year, I attended a writer's conference in San Francisco. Julia Cameron, one of the authors who spoke at the conference, encouraged us each to take time once a week to play. The idea is that play encourages creativity, and creativity fosters our ability to imagine or dream. Returning to the fun of childhood feels silly. The idea of taking a moment out of our day to go swing at the park feels like a waste of time. Pausing our day to visit the penguins at the zoo feels like it might be more trouble than it is worth. But intentional breaks in our busy lives slow us down and allow us to just breathe and enjoy.

Time might feel too short to take your time. Your priorities might not allow a childlike hiatus. But I promise you life is very long when you are miserable or burdened by the weight of regrets.

Life can also be long and oppressive when we act out of emotion rather than considering all of the potential outcomes before we decide how to proceed. In my day job, I often talk about the difference between reacting and responding. Reactions are based solely on emotion. Something happens, and I react automatically without thinking. When someone cuts me off in traffic, for example, I might curse them out. If I am in a hurry, I am more likely to say a few choice words and use a particular hand gesture to let the other driver know how I feel about getting cut off on the highway.

Responses are more level-headed. When we respond we stop and breathe a little bit. Then we consider the consequences or potential outcomes if we respond angrily or with understanding. Responses take a little more time and are designed to create the best possible outcome for everyone involved. Some people call that emotional maturity.

Years ago, I attended church with a woman who regularly poured into my life. She prayed for me and shared the knowledge and understanding she had about life with me. She was a good friend and mentor. I have been known to say exactly what is on my mind, and back then, I was less careful about how I said things. I was not as considerate as I am today. My lack of experience and understanding of life became very obvious when conflict arose. My friend from church pulled me aside one day and said, "Michele, it is the wise woman who ponders." What she meant was that with wisdom came the ability to breathe. Wise women paused, took a breath, and made better decisions than I was making at the time.

If you are going to have the impact in the world that you are destined to have, you must find ways to reclaim your ability to dream and imagine a future beyond what you can imagine now. (There is so much more past what you can imagine!) You have to re-establish the childlike innocence that allows you to find joy in the little things. You must slow down and respond instead of reacting. Lives could be saved if more people paused before moving and took a deep breath.

Slow down.
Stop moving so fast, literally and figuratively.
Do not act in haste. (Make good choices.)
And, breathe.
Please don't forget to breathe.

"Remember to breathe. It is, after all, the secret of life."
Gregory Maguire

Chapter Five

And all that other stuff.

"There's never enough of the stuff you can't get enough of." Patrick H.T. Doyle

Have fun!

Be careful.

Don't drive too fast.

You are who your friends are.

Do you need a hug?

Are you hungry?

You know… stuff like that.

There is so much more I want you to know. But I want to keep this book short and sweet, so here are some quick hits on some other things that I think are important and that I hope you will remember.

Follow directions.

"You don't have to understand directions. All you have to do is follow them, and you can follow them only one step at a time." Louise Dickinson Rich

If directions are in writing, read them all the way through and then read them again. If you don't understand them exactly, ask for help. And if someone is giving you directions out loud, it is ok to ask them to repeat what they said. But say it like, "I'm sorry, I am not clear about what you are asking me to do. Can you repeat that one more time?"

The key is to follow the steps and follow them exactly as they are written or said. DO NOT do it whatever way you would do it because you think your way is faster, smarter, or easier. Follow the directions exactly unless you are told to do "whatever you think is best." You can also ask for permission to do things differently. But make sure you ask before you put your innovative spin on it.

Sometimes following directions is a matter of life and death. Do not die because you could not follow directions or because you refused to follow them.

Be kind.

"Be kind, for everyone you meet is fighting a harder battle." Plato

This should go without saying. Being kind should not be something you have to be told, but we have convinced ourselves that we don't need people, so we are dismissive. Also, being kind takes time, and we rush through life without even paying attention to who is around us.

The word "relationship" is not strictly reserved for intimate situations (i.e., boyfriend/girlfriend, husband/wife, or sexually intimate situations). Relationships are simply the way that people are connected. Relationships go beyond the people who are closest to you.

Whether you realize it or not, you have a relationship with every single person you are in contact with or who you cross paths with over the course of your life. You have a relationship with the person who cuts your hair. If you frequent the same store and you see the same clerk or cashier all the time, you have a relationship with that person. You have a relationship with everyone you go to school with or work with or meet on a regular basis.

Be kind to those people. Let them see how beautiful the world can be in their small and simple encounters with you. Become that friendly face that others look forward to seeing.

Be kind to strangers. Smile, if you feel like it. Sometimes your smile is the only smile a person might see that day. Say hello. Hold the door open for someone. Give a stranger a compliment. Respect others' space. Be patient when you're driving, and someone is walking slowly through the crosswalk in front of you. Wave to your neighbors when you see them outside. Stop at lemonade stands and give those kids a dollar, even if you don't want to drink the lemonade. Be mindful that how you speak to others matters. Look for opportunities in your daily life to be kind.

It will bring joy into your life. It will make you feel good. And, it's contagious. Being kind has the potential to change the world.

Listen and observe.

"What you do with your attention is, in the end what you do with your life." John Green

Listening is a skill that requires practice much like playing an instrument or excelling at a sport. Listening to understand is a much greater challenge than listening so we can respond to someone. When we listen to understand, we consume the words. We take them in, process them, and gain a new perspective, or we reinforce an idea we already had, or we learn something. We absorb the information. We create connections.

When we listen to respond, we gather the information, and we fire back what we know, how we feel, and what we think about the topic. It's hard to restrain ourselves and not respond immediately.

As often as you can, take some time to just listen to everything the same way you listen to music. Listen to hear the words and the sentiment. Listen to hear the story. Listen to the sound of the voices around you, the chirping of the birds, the whisper of the wind on a cool, breezy, sunny day. Listen to the way water trickles in a brook or rushes onto the sand at the beach. Listen to traffic. Listen to the footsteps of people passing by. Listen to the leaves rustling as they tumble across the grass. There is peace in listening. There is understanding in listening. There is clarity in listening.

Observe the world around you. Watch how people interact with one another. Observe the position of their bodies and the language they use in certain situations. If you want to know how to act at a restaurant or the bank or any new situation, watch others. Humble yourself to those who have been there or done that before you. Never assume that you know everything. We all have something to learn. And sometimes the people you give the least amount of credit to have something to teach you.

Pay attention to the mood of every room you walk into. You can see what others are doing, but can you feel the vibe of the space? The mood of the room tells you how you should show up in that space. For example, if the mood is somber or quiet, bursting in loudly might not be appropriate. Or if the mood has a professional tone or feel to it, cursing might not be appropriate. Pay attention and read the room.

Pay attention to what others love, what upsets them, and what brings them joy. Considering someone else's needs and desires is a great way to demonstrate your love for them. Watch how they move, where they gravitate, and how the expression on their faces changes in certain situations. And listen to the little hints they drop in regular conversation that are truly a gateway to getting to know them.

When I was teaching, my kids paid attention to the things I loved because I talked about them all the time. I bet if you asked them now about my favorite things, they could tell you: I love my family. I love dogs.

I love Diet Dr. Pepper, Reese's Peanut Butter Cups, Lay's Dill Pickle Chips, and Dwayne Johnson.

Almost everything you need to know about a person, place, or thing can be discovered through listening and observing.

Use your manners.

"Manners are a sensitive awareness of the feelings of others. If you have that awareness, you have good manners, no matter what fork you use." Emily Post

You might not think that it matters. Or you might think you don't need to do this if the others around you aren't. You might even be one of those folks who say they will not respect others unless they are shown respect first. But I believe that how we act shows who we are, not who others are. And I believe you are better than all of the people walking this earth who are not considerate of the people around them. You are just better than that. Be better than that.

So.. make good use of the following phrases:

Good morning!

Excuse me.

Please.

Thank you.

You're welcome.

Bless you.

If you don't mind…

May I help you?

Have a good day.

I'm sorry.

That last one is a big one. Don't say you are sorry if you don't mean it. Don't say you are sorry if you aren't going to follow through with a change in your behavior. Words have no value if there is no evidence of their meaning in your actions. But if you are sorry, don't wait to say it.

LOVE.

"Being deeply loved by someone gives you strength while loving someone deeply gives you courage." Lao Tzu

Life might not look like it does in the movies with happy endings all the time or ever. You might not feel loved some days. You might feel rejected or abandoned. But somewhere, somebody loves you. But, if you are struggling to see it or to find that person right now, please know that ***I love you***.

Love is complicated. I don't care what anyone else says about it. Sometimes we seek validation or love from people who are not equipped to give it to us. And sometimes, the people we love don't love us in the same way that we love them. That can leave us feeling unworthy or not valued.

Some of us set the bar of expectations so high for the people that actually do love us that it's impossible for them to meet those expectations. Or we build emotional walls to protect our hearts, our spirits, our whole beings. But we are blocking out the goodness and light that is being sent to us by safe, nurturing people.

Maybe you have convinced yourself that if people knew the real you, if they knew the things you have done or the thoughts you have had, they would not love you. You may have decided, because of your past, your circumstances, that you are not loveable. Or maybe someone has actually told you that you are not easy to love. I have felt unworthy and undervalued and not easy to love too.

We don't always get what we want or need from the people we want or need it from, and that often leads us to feel like we don't need anybody. But the truth is relationships are the foundation of every success you will ever have. They are the key to changing the trajectory of your trauma. They are an integral part of our journey as humans. We need people.

Do not be afraid to love. Do not be afraid to let other people love you. You deserve to be loved. Not just liked. Not just wanted or lusted after, or objectified. You deserve to be loved wholly and completely.

I am not going to lie to you and tell you that it will be wonderful and perfect and all roses and rainbows and ice cream and sunny days. There will be disappointments. There will be heartbreak. Lessons learned often come in the form of relationships gone wrong.

When it comes to romantic love, I have not always been successful. I am not ashamed to admit that. Many of the failures in my relationships have been solely my fault and responsibility. (And the rest of them are because I am really good at picking the wrong people!) But I have found joy in every relationship I have been in.

I remember a time when I felt embarrassed because I felt so loved. My boyfriend, at that time, focused intently on my face when I talked. He not only listened to the sound of my voice, but he heard me. One day, after a long conversation, I realized I had been going on and on about something I really believed in. When I looked up, he smiled and said, "You are so beautiful when you talk about what you do because you love it so much." And I thought, "Wow, that man loves me." He would listen to me for hours. He paid attention to me. He found happiness in my presence. "I love you" is just words if there are no actions to support them. He showed me every day that he loved me. He didn't just say it.

I have also struggled with friendships at times. Part of my struggle in relationships is due to my inherent sense of abandonment. That means that I believe that everyone is going to leave me. So, I work really hard to push people out of my life before they can leave on their own. Sometimes I make it impossible for people to love me, and it even makes me tired.

But I do keep trying no matter how many times I say, "Never again!" I keep trying to meet people where they are and spend time with them doing the things I mentioned throughout this book, like observing and listening, and learning. And, I am grateful that love is not limited to romance or intimacy.

In fact, love is limitless. You don't have to have it in reserve to give it. Love exists bountifully within you.

It just takes some time to find it or to pull it up to the surface sometimes. You were created with a great capacity to love and to receive love.

I love hard. I love my friends and my family, my students, and my neighbors. I love my colleagues and my teammates, and the people I meet in various aspects of my life as deeply and wholly as I can. And they love me back in the best way they each know how.

That's another part of loving people… Understanding what they are capable of giving you and being ok with that. Not everyone will love as you love. But they will still love you in their way, the best they can. We must recognize when someone is loving the best way they know how because it is love.

I tend to seek out the good in people. Usually, I can see how they love who they love, and I admire that. Oddly enough, I seem to have the easiest time seeing the good and beautiful things in the people who hate me. I am grateful for that ability because it helps me not to hate in return. (Hate feels so ugly on the inside.)

When you are able to tap into your love reserve, it makes life so much more glorious. And suddenly, you find yourself loving the way your coffee tastes in the morning or the way the sun sets just outside your window in the evening. Beauty will leap out at you in crowds of people, and your taste for music and, food and, art, and everything else will become crisper, clearer, cleaner. Love and loving changes you completely.

Love with all you've got. Even when it's hard to do. And say it. Say "I love you" every chance you get because you never know when it will be the last chance you have. Say it to yourself every day. And if you are just not there yet. Then read it right here, anytime you need to:

I LOVE YOU.

www.ingramcontent.com/pod-product-compliance
Lightning Source LLC
Chambersburg PA
CBHW071448150726

48000CB00006B/2487